D0688217

Critical Acclaim for
In the Name of Jesus

"*In the Name of Jesus* draws provocative and stimulating conclusions about the meaning and significance of Christian ministry." — *Christianity Today*

"One of the most powerful books I have read in a long time." — *Deacon Digest*

"Anyone involved in Christian ministry needs to read this book." — *The Theological Educator*

"An incisive, moving book." — *Review and Expositor*

"Nouwen writes succinctly, with clarity and ease." — *Sojourners*

"An absolute treasure. There is more packed between the covers of this little book that adults will find helpful to living a Christian life than you'll find in many a volume three times its size." — *Our Sunday Visitor*

"It will not take you long to read this excellent little book, but be prepared for it to occupy your thoughts for quite a while." — *Chattanooga Times*

"A small but powerful volume about ministry." — *Catholic Book Club*

"Although the book's subtitle indicates that it is directed towards leaders, the message is more universal.... A wonderful book." — *NPH*

"He packs in more wisdom than most authors do in books ten times the size." — *Leadership*

"Although he is addressing those who in one way or another are in a leadership role, this simple, Gospel-based message is relevant to everyone." — *Prairie Messenger*

"With passion and intelligence, Nouwen speaks to the current 'crisis in ministry,' offering a powerful apologetic for Christian ministry." — *Restoration Quarterly*

"Nouwen's trademark honesty and compassion permeate every page. . . . Every church library should have a Nouwen collection, and this title should be in it."
— *Church and Synagogue Library Association*

"The overall message of the book is as touching and moving as we have seen before in Nouwen's work. The image of the servant-leader among the people is one that needs to be pointed out again and again in the church."
— *Sisters Today*

"A jewel." — *Catholic Twin Circle*

"Savor the insights of a gifted writer, a deep thinker, and, above all, a lover of Jesus." — *Christian Home and School*

"These reflections come out of his own openness to personal struggle and growth — in this case, recent experiences as priest at a L'Arche community for the mentally handicapped. . . . His message movingly conveys how his relationships with these broken people have touched him deeply in return. Heart-warming and provocative." — *Library Journal*

In the Name *of* Jesus

HENRI J.M. NOUWEN

In the Name *of* Jesus

REFLECTIONS ON
CHRISTIAN LEADERSHIP

with study guide
for groups and individuals

A Crossroad Book
The Crossroad Publishing Company
New York

The Crossroad Publishing Company
481 Eighth Avenue, New York, NY 10001

Library of Congress Cataloging-in-Publication Data

Nouwen, Henri J. M.
    In the name of Jesus : reflections on Christian leadership
    / Henri J. M. Nouwen.
        p. cm.
    ISBN 0-8245-0915-3; 0-8245-1259-6 (pbk).
    1. Christian leadership. I. Title.
    BV652.1.N68 1989
    262'.1 – dc19
                                            88-32620

    3 4 5 6 7 8 9 10   08 07 06 05 04

To Murray McDonnell

Contents

Acknowledgments

In the preparation of this little book I have received invaluable help. I would like especially to express my gratitude to Connie Ellis for her secretarial assistance, to Conrad Wieczorek for his skillful editing of the manuscript, and to Sue Mosteller for her insightful comments on the content. I also want to say thanks to Bob Heller, the president of Crossroad, who was the first to suggest publication of this text in book form.

The most encouraging and life-giving response to *In the Name of Jesus* came from Gordon Cosby and Diana Chambers of the Church of the Saviour in Washington, D.C.

They told me that their new Servant Leadership School is trying to form Christian leaders based on the vision expressed in these pages. The Servant Leadership School wants to nurture a Christian leadership in which a life of prayer, confession, and forgiveness in community is intimately united with a life of ministry among the inner-city poor.

The Servant Leadership School offers a unique opportunity to pursue a spiritual journey in which unceasing prayer and committed service can be lived as the two inseparable qualities of the call of Jesus.

I am deeply grateful to know that what is written here is finding a very concrete expression in a new school of Christian discipleship.

Prologue

When my friend Murray McDonnell visited me at the Daybreak community near Toronto, he asked me whether I would be willing to speak about Christian leadership in the twenty-first century, the occasion being the fifteenth anniversary of the Center for Human Development in Washington, D.C. Although I had only recently begun my work as a priest at Daybreak, one of the L'Arche communities for mentally handicapped people, I did not want to disappoint Murray, who, as chairman of the board of the Center for Human Development, had given much of his time and energy to its growth. I also knew Father Vincent Dwyer, the Center's founder, and had great admiration for his dedicated work in helping priests and ministers in their search for emotional and spiritual wholeness. So I said yes.

But after having said yes to the invitation, I realized that it was far from easy to come up with a sane perspective on Christian leadership for the twenty-first century. The audience would mostly be priests who were themselves deeply involved in ministry to their fellow priests. What would I be able to say to people who are thinking day in and day out about the future of the priesthood and the ministry in the church? I also wondered how it would be possible to look ahead of me, into the new century, when I considered that nobody in the 1950s could have foreseen the situation of most priests today. Still, the more I said to myself, "I can't do this," the more I discovered within me a desire to put into words my thoughts about ministry as they had evolved since my joining the Daybreak community. For many years I had taught courses about ministry. Now, having stepped away from the academic life and having been called to be a priest for mentally handicapped people and their assistants, I asked myself, "How do I now live from day to day after having spoken for twenty years to young men and women preparing themselves for ministry? How do I think about my ministry and how do these thoughts affect my everyday words and actions?"

I also came to see that I should not worry about tomorrow, next week, next year, or the next century. The more willing I was to look honestly at what I was thinking and saying and doing now, the more easily I would come into touch with the movement of God's Spirit in me, leading me to the future. God is a God of the present and reveals to those who are willing to listen carefully to the moment in which they live the steps they are to take toward the future. "Do not worry about tomorrow," Jesus says. "Tomorrow will take care of itself. Each day has enough trouble of its own" (Matthew 6:34).

With these thoughts, I began to write down what I most deeply felt about my present life as a priest at Daybreak, trying carefully to discern which of my own experiences and insights could speak to priests and ministers who live in very

Jesus did not send his disciples out alone to preach the word. He sent them two by two.

different circumstances. The present work is the result.

Before concluding these introductory remarks, however, I must tell you, the readers of this little book, that I did not go to Washington, D.C., by myself. As I was preparing my presentation, I became deeply aware of the fact that Jesus did not send his disciples out alone to preach the word. He sent them two by two. I began to wonder why nobody was planning to go with me. If my present life is truly a life among handicapped people, why not ask one of them to join me on the journey and to share the ministry with me?

After some consultation, the Daybreak community decided to send Bill Van Buren with me. Since my arrival at Daybreak, Bill and I had become good friends. Of all the handicapped people in the house, he was the most able to express himself with words and gestures. From the beginning of our friendship, he had shown a real interest in my work as a priest and had offered to help me during services. One day he told me that he had not been baptized and expressed a strong desire to belong to the church. I suggested that he join a parish program for those who desired baptism. Faithfully he went to the local parish every Thursday evening. Even though the long and often complex presentations and discussions were far beyond his mental capacities, he had a real sense of belonging to the group. He felt accepted and loved. He received much and, with his generous heart, gave much in return. His Baptism, Confirmation, and First Communion during the Easter Vigil became a real high point in his life. While limited in his ability to express himself in many words, he felt deeply touched by Jesus and knew what it meant to be reborn by water and the Holy Spirit.

Often I had told Bill that those who are baptized and confirmed have a new vocation, the vocation to proclaim to others the good news of Jesus. Bill had listened to me carefully, and when I invited him to go with me to Washington, D.C., to speak to priests and ministers, he accepted it as an invitation to join me in my ministry. "We are doing this together," he said at different times in the days before we left.

"Yes," I kept saying, "we are doing this together. You and I are going to Washington to proclaim the Gospel."

Bill did not for a moment doubt the truth of this. While I was quite nervous about what to say and how to say it, Bill showed great confidence in his task. And, while I was still thinking about Bill's trip with me primarily as something that would be nice for him, Bill was, from the beginning, convinced that he was going to help me. I later came to realize that he knew better than I. As we stepped on board the plane in Toronto, Bill reminded me again, "We are doing this together, aren't we?"

"Yes, Bill," I said, "we sure are."

After telling you what I said in Washington, I will tell you in more detail what happened there and explain to you why Bill's presence most likely had a more lasting influence than my words.

Introduction

The request to reflect on Christian leadership in the new century has created quite a bit of anxiety in me. What can I say about the twenty-first century if I feel at a loss when people ask me about next month? After a lot of inner turmoil, I decided to stay as close to my own heart as possible. I asked myself, "What decisions have you been making lately and how are they a reflection of the way you sense the future?" Somehow I have to trust that God is at work in me and that the way I am being moved to new inner and outer places is part of a larger movement of which I am only a very small part.

After twenty years in the academic world as a teacher of pastoral psychology, pastoral theology, and Christian spirituality, I began to experience a deep inner threat. As I entered into my fifties and was able to realize the unlikelihood of doubling my years, I came face to face with the simple question, "Did becoming older bring me closer to Jesus?" After twenty-five years of priesthood, I found myself praying poorly, living somewhat isolated from other people, and very much preoccupied with burning issues. Everyone was saying that I was doing really well, but something inside was telling me that my success was putting my own soul in danger. I began to ask myself whether my lack of contemplative prayer, my loneliness, and my constantly changing involvement in what seemed most urgent were signs that the Spirit was gradually being suppressed. It was very hard for me to see clearly, and though I never spoke about hell or only jokingly so, I woke up one day with the realization that I was living in a very dark place and that the term "burnout" was a convenient psychological translation for a spiritual death.

In the midst of this I kept praying, "Lord, show me where you want me to go and I will follow

I was living in a very dark place and the term "burnout" was a convenient psychological translation for a spiritual death.

you, but please be clear and unambiguous about it!" Well, God was. In the person of Jean Vanier, the founder of the L'Arche communities for men-tally handicapped people, God said, "Go and live among the poor in spirit, and they will heal you." The call was so clear and distinct that I had no choice but to follow.

So I moved from Harvard to L'Arche, from the best and the brightest, wanting to rule the world, to men and women who had few or no words and were considered, at best, marginal to the needs of our society. It was a very hard and painful move, and I am still in the process of making it. After twenty years of being free to go where I wanted and to discuss what I chose, the small, hidden life with people whose broken minds and bodies demand a strict daily routine in which words are the least requirement does not immediately ap-pear as the solution for spiritual burnout. And yet, my new life at L'Arche is offering me new words to use in speaking about Christian leader-ship in the future because I have found there all the challenges that we are facing as ministers of God's Word.

So I will offer you some images from my life with people with a mental handicap. I hope that they will give you some inkling of the direction to take when wondering about Christian leadership in the future. In sharing my reflections with you, I will be guided by two stories from the Gospels: the story of Jesus' temptation in the desert (Matthew 4:1–11) and the story of Peter's call to be a shepherd (John 21:15–19).

I

From Relevance to Prayer

"One does not live by bread alone, but by every word that comes from the mouth of God."

The Temptation:
To Be Relevant

The first thing that struck me when I came to live in a house with mentally handicapped people was that their liking or disliking me had absolutely nothing to do with any of the many useful things I had done until then. Since nobody could read my books, the books could not impress anyone, and since most of them never went to school, my twenty years at Notre Dame, Yale, and Harvard did not provide a significant introduction. My considerable [ecumenical] experience proved even less valuable. When I offered some meat to one of the assistants during dinner, one of the

[representing]
a number of
Christian Churches

handicapped men said to me, "Don't give him meat. He doesn't eat meat. He's a Presbyterian."

Not being able to use any of the skills that had proved so practical in the past was a real source of anxiety. I was suddenly faced with my naked self, open for affirmations and rejections, hugs and punches, smiles and tears, all dependent simply on how I was perceived at the moment. In a way, it seemed as though I was starting my life all over again. Relationships, connections, reputations could no longer be counted on.

This experience was and, in many ways, is still the most important experience of my new life, because it forced me to rediscover my true identity. These broken, wounded, and completely unpretentious people forced me to let go of my relevant self — the self that can do things, show things, prove things, build things — and forced me to reclaim that unadorned self in which I am completely vulnerable, open to receive and give love regardless of any accomplishments.

I am telling you all this because I am deeply

I was suddenly faced with my naked self, open for affirmations and rejections, hugs and punches, smiles and tears, all dependent simply on how I was perceived at the moment.

convinced that the Christian leader of the future is called to be completely irrelevant and to stand in this world with nothing to offer but his or her own vulnerable self. That is the way Jesus came to reveal God's love. The great message that we have to carry, as ministers of God's Word and followers of Jesus, is that God loves us not because of what we do or accomplish, but because God has created and redeemed us in love and has chosen us to proclaim that love as the true source of all human life.

Jesus' first temptation was to be relevant: to turn stones into bread. Oh, how often have I wished I could do that! Walking through the "young towns" on the outskirts of Lima, Peru, where children die from malnutrition and contaminated water, I would not have been able to reject the magical gift of making the dusty stone-covered streets into places where people could pick up any of the thousands of rocks and discover that they were croissants, coffee cakes, or fresh-baked buns, and where they could fill their cupped hands with stale water from the cisterns and joyfully realize that what they were drinking was delicious milk. Aren't we priests and ministers called to help people, to feed the hungry, and to save those who are starving? Are we not called to do something that makes people realize that we do make a difference in their lives? Aren't we called to heal the sick, feed the hungry, and alleviate the suffering of the poor? Jesus was faced with these same questions, but when he was asked to prove his power as the Son of God by the relevant behavior of changing stones into bread, he clung to his mission to proclaim the Word and said, "One does not live by bread alone, but by every word that comes from the mouth of God" (Matthew 4:4).

One of the main sufferings experienced in the ministry is that of low self-esteem. Many priests and ministers today increasingly perceive themselves as having very little impact. They are very busy, but they do not see much change. It seems that their efforts are fruitless. They face an ongoing decrease in church attendance and discover that psychologists, psychotherapists, marriage counselors, and doctors are often more trusted than they. One of the most painful realizations for many Christian leaders is that fewer and fewer young people feel attracted to follow in their footsteps. It might seem that nowadays, becoming and being a priest or minister is no longer something worth dedicating your life to. Meanwhile, there is little praise and much criticism in the church today, and who can live for long in such a climate without slipping into some type of depression?

The secular world around us is saying in a loud voice, "We can take care of ourselves. We do not need God, the church, or a priest. We are in control. And if we are not, then we have to work harder to get in control. The problem is not lack of faith, but lack of competence. If you are sick, you need a competent doctor; if you are poor, you need competent politicians; if there are technical problems, you need competent engineers; if there

Self —
sufficiency
is respectable
+
admired

are wars, you need competent negotiators. God, the church, and the minister have been used for centuries to fill the gaps of incompetence, but to-day the gaps are being filled in other ways, and we no longer need spiritual answers to practical questions."

In this climate of secularization, Christian leaders feel less and less relevant and more and more marginal. Many begin to wonder why they should stay in the ministry. Often they leave, develop a new competency, and join their con-temporaries in their attempts to make relevant contributions to a better world.

But there is a completely different story to tell. Beneath all the great accomplishments of our time there is a deep current of despair. While efficiency and control are the great aspirations of our society, the loneliness, isolation, lack of friendship and intimacy, broken relationships, boredom, feelings of emptiness and depression, and a deep sense of uselessness fill the hearts of millions of people in our success-oriented world.

Bret Easton Ellis's novel *Less Than Zero* offers a most graphic description of the moral and spiritual poverty behind the contemporary facade of wealth, success, popularity, and power. In a dramatically staccato way, he describes the life of sex, drugs, and violence among the teenage sons and daughters of the super-rich entertainers in Los Angeles. And the cry that arises from behind all of this decadence is clearly: "Is there anybody who loves me? Is there anybody who really cares? Is there anybody who wants to stay home for me? Is there anybody who wants to be with me when I am not in control, when I feel like crying? Is there anybody who can hold me and give me a sense of belonging?" Feeling irrelevant is a much more general experience than we might think when we look at our seemingly self-confident society. Medical technology and the tragic increase in abortions may radically diminish the number of mentally handicapped people in our society, but it is already becoming apparent that more and more people are suffering from profound moral and spiritual handicaps without having any idea of where to look for healing.

It is here that the need for a new Christian leadership becomes clear. The leaders of the future will be those who dare to claim their irrelevance in the contemporary world as a divine vocation that allows them to enter into a deep solidarity with the anguish underlying all the glitter of success, and to bring the light of Jesus there.

The Question: "Do You Love Me?"

Before Jesus commissioned Peter to be a shepherd, he asked him, "Simon, son of John, do you love me more than these others do?" He asked him again, "Do you love me?" And a third time he asked: "Do you love me?" (John 21:15–17). We have to hear that question as being central to all of our Christian ministry because it is the question that can allow us to be, at the same time, irrelevant and truly self-confident.

Look at Jesus. The world did not pay any attention to him. He was crucified and put away. His message of love was rejected by a world in ier for people to recognize that we do not come in our own name, but in the name of the Lord Jesus who sent us.

In the past I traveled a lot, preaching and giving retreats as well as commencement and keynote addresses. But I always went alone. Now, however, every time I am sent by the community to speak somewhere, the community tries to send me with a companion. Being with Bill is a concrete expression of the vision that we should not only live in community, but also minister in community. Bill and I were sent by our community in the conviction that the same Lord who binds us together in love will also reveal himself to us and others as we walk together on the road.

But there is more. Ministry is not only a communal experience, it is also a mutual experience. Jesus, speaking about his own shepherding ministry, says, "I am the good shepherd. I know my own and my own know me, just as the Father knows me and I know the Father; and I lay down my life for my sheep" (John 10:14–15). As Jesus search of power, efficiency, and control. But there he was, appearing with wounds in his glorified body to a few friends who had eyes to see, ears to hear, and hearts to understand. This rejected, unknown, wounded Jesus simply asked, "Do you love me, do you really love me?" He whose only concern had been to announce the unconditional love of God had only one question to ask, "Do you love me?"

The question is not: How many people take you seriously? How much are you going to accomplish? Can you show some results? But: Are you in love with Jesus? Perhaps another way of putting the question would be: Do you know the incarnate God? In our world of loneliness and despair, there is an enormous need for men and women who know the heart of God, a heart that forgives, cares, reaches out and wants to heal. In that heart there is no suspicion, no vindictiveness, no resentment, and not a tinge of hatred. It is a heart that wants only to give love and receive love in response. It is a heart that suffers immensely because it sees the magnitude of human pain and the great resistance to trusting the heart of God who wants to offer consolation and hope.

The Christian leader of the future is the one who truly knows the heart of God as it has become flesh, "a heart of flesh," in Jesus. Knowing God's heart means consistently, radically, and very concretely to announce and reveal that God is love and only love, and that every time fear, isolation, or despair begins to invade the human soul, this is not something that comes from God. This sounds very simple and maybe even trite, but very few people know that they are loved without any conditions or limits.

This unconditional and unlimited love is what the evangelist John calls God's first love. "Let us love," he says, "because God loved us first" (1 John 4:19). The love that often leaves us doubtful, frustrated, angry, and resentful is the second love, that is to say, the affirmation, affection, sympathy, encouragement, and support

The Christian leader of the future is the one who truly knows the heart of God as it has become flesh, "a heart of flesh," in Jesus.

we receive from our parents, teachers, spouses, and friends. We all know how limited, broken, and very fragile that love is. Behind the many expressions of this second love there is always the chance of rejection, withdrawal, punishment, blackmail, violence, and even hatred. Many contemporary movies and plays portray the ambiguities and ambivalences of human relationships, and there are no friendships, marriages, or communities in which the strains and stresses of the second love are not keenly felt. Often it seems that beneath the pleasantries of daily life there are many gaping wounds that carry such names as abandonment, betrayal, rejection, rupture, and loss. These are all the shadow side of the second love and reveal the darkness that never completely leaves the human heart.

The radical good news is that the second love is only a broken reflection of the first love and that the first love is offered to us by a God in whom there are no shadows. Jesus' heart is the incarnation of the shadow-free first love of God. From his heart flow streams of living water. He cries out in a loud voice, "Let anyone who is thirsty come to me! Let anyone who believes in me come and drink" (John 7:37–38). "Come to me, all you who labor and are overburdened, and I will give you rest. Shoulder my yoke and learn from me, for I am gentle and humble in heart and you will find rest for your souls" (Matthew 11:28–29).

From that heart come the words, "Do you love me?" Knowing the heart of Jesus and loving him are the same thing. The knowledge of Jesus' heart is a knowledge of the heart. And when we live in the world with that knowledge, we cannot do other than bring healing, reconciliation, new life, and hope wherever we go. The desire to be relevant and successful will gradually disappear, and our only desire will be to say with our whole being to our brothers and sisters of the human race, "You are loved. There is no reason to be afraid. In love God created your inmost self and knit you together in your mother's womb" (see Psalm 139:13).

The Discipline: Contemplative Prayer

To live a life that is not dominated by the desire to be relevant but is instead safely anchored in the knowledge of God's first love, we have to be mystics. A mystic is a person whose identity is deeply rooted in God's first love.

If there is any focus that the Christian leader of the future will need, it is the discipline of dwelling in the presence of the One who keeps asking us, "Do you love me? Do you love me? Do you love me?" This is the discipline of contemplative prayer. Through contemplative prayer we can keep ourselves from being pulled from one urgent issue to another and from becoming strangers to our own heart and God's heart. Contemplative prayer keeps us home, rooted and safe, even when we are on the road, moving from place to place, and often surrounded by sounds of violence and war. Contemplative prayer deepens in us the knowledge that we are already free, that we have already found a place to dwell, that we already belong to God, even though everything and everyone around us keep suggesting the opposite.

It is not enough for the priests and ministers of the future to be moral people, well trained, eager to help their fellow humans, and able to respond creatively to the burning issues of their time. All of that is very valuable and important, but it is not the heart of Christian leadership. The central question is, Are the leaders of the future truly men and women of God, people with an ardent desire to dwell in God's presence, to listen to God's voice, to look at God's beauty, to touch God's incarnate Word, and to taste fully God's infinite goodness?

The original meaning of the word "theology" was "union with God in prayer." Today theology has become one academic discipline alongside many others, and often theologians are finding it hard to pray. But for the future of Christian leadership it is of vital importance to reclaim the mystical aspect of theology so that every word spoken, every word of advice given, and every strategy developed can come from a heart that knows God intimately. I have the impression that many of the debates within the church around issues such as the papacy, the ordination of women, the marriage of priests, homosexuality, birth control, abortion, and euthanasia take place on a primarily moral level. On that level, different parties battle about right or wrong. But that battle is often removed from the experience of God's first love, which lies at the base of all human relationships.

Words like "right-wing," "reactionary," "conservative," "liberal," and "left-wing" are used to describe people's opinions, and many discussions then seem more like political battles for power than spiritual searches for the truth.

Christian leaders cannot simply be persons who have well-informed opinions about the burning issues of our time. Their leadership must be rooted in the permanent, intimate relationship with the incarnate Word, Jesus, and they need to find there the source for their words, advice, and guidance. Through the discipline of contemplative prayer, Christian leaders have to learn to listen again and again to the voice of love and to find there the wisdom and courage to address whatever issue presents itself to them. Dealing with burning issues without being rooted in a deep personal relationship with God easily leads to divisiveness because, before we know it, our sense of self is caught up in our opinion about a given subject. But when we are securely rooted in personal intimacy with the source of life, it will be possible to remain flexible without being relativistic, convinced without being rigid, willing to confront without being offensive, gentle and

Christian leaders cannot simply be persons who have well-informed opinions about the burning issues of our time.

forgiving without being soft, and true witnesses without being manipulative.

For Christian leadership to be truly fruitful in the future, a movement from the moral to the mystical is required.

• 47 •

has invested so much, but the way of downward mobility ending on the cross. This might sound morbid and masochistic, but for those who have heard the voice of the first love and said yes to it, the downward-moving way of Jesus is the way to the joy and the peace of God, a joy and peace that is not of this world.

Here we touch the most important quality of Christian leadership in the future. It is not a leadership of power and control, but a leadership of powerlessness and humility in which the suffering servant of God, Jesus Christ, is made manifest. I, obviously, am not speaking about a psychologically weak leadership in which Christian leaders are simply the passive victims of the manipulations of their milieu. No, I am speaking of a leadership in which power is constantly abandoned in favor of love. It is a true spiritual leadership. Powerlessness and humility in the spiritual life do not refer to people who have no spine and who let everyone else make decisions for them. They refer to people who are

II

From Popularity to Ministry

*"Feed my lambs,
look after my sheep"*

The Temptation: To Be Spectacular

Let me tell you about another experience that came out of my move from Harvard to L'Arche. It was the experience of shared ministry. I was educated in a seminary that made me believe ministry was essentially an individual affair. I had to be well trained and well formed, and after six years of training and formation, I was considered well equipped to preach, administer the sacraments, counsel, and run a parish. I was made to feel like a man sent on a long, long hike with a huge backpack containing all the things necessary to help the people I would meet on the road.

Questions had answers, problems had solutions, and pains had their medicines. Just be sure that you know with which one of the three you are dealing. Over the years, I realized that things are not as simple as that, but my basic individualistic approach to ministry did not change. When I became a teacher I was even more encouraged to do my own thing. I could choose my own subject, my own method, and sometimes even my own students. Nobody would even question my way of doing things. And when I left the classroom I was completely free to do whatever I saw fit. After all, we all have a right to live our private lives privately!

When I went to L'Arche, however, this individualism was radically challenged. There I was one of many people who tried to live faithfully with handicapped people, and the fact that I was a priest was not a license to do things on my own. Suddenly everyone wanted to know my whereabouts from hour to hour, and every movement I made was subject to accountability. One member of the community was appointed to accompany me; a small group was formed to help me decide which invitations to accept and which to decline; and the question most asked by the handicapped people with whom I live was, "Are you home to-night?" Once, when I had left on a trip without saying goodbye to Trevor, one of the handicapped people with whom I live, the first phone call I received when I had reached my destination was a tearful call from Trevor, saying, "Henri, why did you leave us? We miss you so. Please come back."

Living in a community with very wounded people, I came to see that I had lived most of my life as a tightrope artist trying to walk on a high, thin cable from one tower to the other, always waiting for the applause when I had not fallen off and broken my leg.

The second temptation to which Jesus was exposed was precisely the temptation to do some-thing spectacular, something that could win him great applause. "Throw yourself from the parapet of the temple and let the angels catch you

Jesus refused to be a stunt man. He did not come to walk on hot coals, swallow fire, or put his hand in the lion's mouth to demonstrate that he had something worthwhile to say.

and carry you in their arms" (see Matthew 4:6). But Jesus refused to be a stunt man. He did not come to prove himself. He did not come to walk on hot coals, swallow fire, or put his hand in the lion's mouth to demonstrate that he had something worthwhile to say. "Don't put the Lord your God to the test," he said.

When you look at today's church, it is easy to see the prevalence of individualism among ministers and priests. Not too many of us have a vast repertoire of skills to be proud of, but most of us still feel that, if we have anything at all to show, it is something we have to do solo. You could say that many of us feel like failed tightrope walkers who discovered that we did not have the power to draw thousands of people, that we could not make many conversions, that we did not have the talents to create beautiful liturgies, that we were not as popular with the youth, the young adults, or the elderly as we had hoped, and that we were not as able to respond to the needs of our people as we had expected. But most of us still feel that, ideally, we should have been able to do it all and do it successfully. Stardom and individual heroism, which are such obvious aspects of our competitive society, are not at all alien to the church. There too the dominant image is that of the self-made man or woman who can do it all alone.

The Task: "Feed My Sheep"

After having asked Peter three times, "Do you love me?" Jesus says, "Feed my lambs, look after my sheep, feed my sheep." Having been assured of Peter's love, Jesus gives him the task of ministry. In the context of our own culture we might hear this in a very individualistic way, as if Peter now was being sent on a heroic mission. But when Jesus speaks about shepherding, he does not want us to think about a brave, lonely shepherd who takes care of a large flock of obedient sheep. In many ways, he makes it clear that ministry is a communal and mutual experience.

First of all, Jesus sends the twelve out in pairs
(Mark 6:7). We keep forgetting that we are being sent out two-by-two. We cannot bring good
news on our own. We are called to proclaim the
Gospel together, in community. There is a divine
wisdom here. "If two of you on earth agree to ask
anything at all, it will be granted to you by my
Father in heaven. For where two or three meet
in my name, I am there among them" (Matthew
18:19–20). You might already have discovered for
yourself how radically different traveling alone is
from traveling together. I have found over and
over again how hard it is to be truly faithful to
Jesus when I am alone. I need my brothers or
sisters to pray with me, to speak with me about
the spiritual task at hand, and to challenge me to
stay pure in mind, heart, and body. But far more
importantly, it is Jesus who heals, not I; Jesus who
speaks words of truth, not I; Jesus who is Lord,
not I. This is very clearly made visible when we
proclaim the redeeming power of God together.
Indeed, whenever we minister together, it is eas-

It is Jesus who heals, not I; Jesus who speaks words of truth, not I; Jesus who is Lord, not I.

ministers, so he wants us to minister. He wants Peter to feed his sheep and care for them, not as "professionals" who know their clients' problems and take care of them, but as vulnerable brothers and sisters who know and are known, who care and are cared for, who forgive and are being forgiven, who love and are being loved.

Somehow we have come to believe that good leadership requires a safe distance from those we are called to lead. Medicine, psychiatry, and social work all offer us models in which "service" takes place in a one-way direction. Someone serves, someone else is being served, and be sure not to mix up the roles! But how can we lay down our life for those with whom we are not even allowed to enter into a deep personal relationship? Laying down your life means making your own faith and doubt, hope and despair, joy and sadness, courage and fear available to others as ways of getting in touch with the Lord of life.

We are not the healers, we are not the reconcilers, we are not the givers of life. We are sinful, broken, vulnerable people who need as much care as anyone we care for. The mystery of ministry is that we have been chosen to make our own limited and very conditional love the gateway for the unlimited and unconditional love of God.

Therefore, true ministry must be mutual. When the members of a community of faith cannot truly know and love their shepherd, shepherding quickly becomes a subtle way of exercising power over others and begins to show authoritarian and dictatorial traits. The world in which we live — a world of efficiency and control — has no models to offer to those who want to be shepherds in the way Jesus was a shepherd. Even the so-called "helping professions" have been so thoroughly secularized that mutuality can only be seen as a weakness and a dangerous form of role confusion. The leadership about which Jesus speaks is of a radically different kind from the leadership offered by the world. It is a servant leadership — to use Robert Greenleaf's term* — in which the leader is a vulnerable servant who needs the people as much as they need their leader.

From this it is clear that a whole new type of leadership is asked for in the church of tomorrow, a leadership that is not modeled on the power games of the world, but on the servant-leader Jesus, who came to give his life for the salvation of many.

---

*Robert K. Greenleaf, *Servant Leadership: A Journey into the Nature of Legitimate Power and Greatness* (New York: Paulist Press, 1977). See also Robert K. Greenleaf, *The Power of Servant-Leadership* (San Francisco: Berrett-Koehler Publishers, 1998).

The Discipline:
Confession and Forgiveness

Having said this, we are faced with the question: What discipline is required for the future leader to overcome the temptation of individual heroism? I would like to propose the discipline of confession and forgiveness. Just as the future leaders must be mystics deeply steeped in contemplative prayer, so also must they be persons always willing to confess their own brokenness and ask for forgiveness from those to whom they minister.

Confession and forgiveness are the concrete forms in which we sinful people love one another. Often I have the impression that priests and ministers are the least confessing people in the Christian community. The sacrament of Confession has often become a way to keep our own vulnerability hidden from our community. Sins are mentioned and ritual words of forgiveness are spoken, but seldom does a real encounter take place in which the reconciling and healing presence of Jesus can be experienced. There is so much fear, so much distance, so much generalization, and so little real listening, speaking, and absolving that not much true sacramentality can be expected.

How can priests or ministers feel really loved and cared for when they have to hide their own sins and failings from the people to whom they minister and run off to a distant stranger to receive a little comfort and consolation? How can people truly care for their shepherds and keep them faithful to their sacred task when they do not know them and so cannot deeply love them? I am not at all surprised that so many ministers built on power to a leadership in which we critically discern where God is leading us and our people.

The people of L'Arche are showing me new ways. I am a slow learner. Old patterns that have proved quite effective are not easy to give up. But as I think about the Christian leader of the twenty-first century, I do believe that those from whom I least expected to learn are showing me the way. I hope and pray that what I am learning in my new life is something that is not just good for me to learn, but something that helps you, as well, to catch a glimpse of the Christian leader of the future.

What I have said is, obviously, nothing new, but I hope and pray that you have seen that the oldest, most traditional vision of Christian leadership is still a vision that awaits realization in the future.

I leave you with the image of the leader with outstretched hands, who chooses a life of downward mobility. It is the image of the praying

*How can people truly care for their shepherds
and keep them faithful to their sacred task
when they do not know them and so cannot
deeply love them?*

and priests suffer immensely from deep emotional loneliness, frequently feel a great need for affectivity and intimacy, and sometimes experience a deep-seated guilt and shame in front of their own people. Often they seem to say, "What if my people knew how I really feel, what I think and daydream about, and where my mind wanders when I am sitting by myself in my study?"

It is precisely the men and women who are dedicated to spiritual leadership who are easily subject to very raw carnality. The reason for this is that they do not know how to live the truth of the Incarnation. They separate themselves from their own concrete community, try to deal with their needs by ignoring them or satisfying them in distant or anonymous places, and then experience an increasing split between their own most private inner world and the good news they announce. When spirituality becomes spiritualization, life in the body becomes carnality. When ministers and priests live their ministry mostly in their heads and relate to the Gospel as a set of

Bill looked at me attentively and then said, "And we did it together, didn't we?"

Then I realized the full truth of Jesus' words, "Where two or three meet in my Name, I am among them" (Matthew 18:20). In the past, I had always given lectures, sermons, addresses, and speeches by myself. Often I had wondered how much of what I had said would be remembered. Now it dawned on me that most likely much of what I said would not be long remembered, but that Bill and I doing it together would not easily be forgotten. I hoped and prayed that Jesus, who had sent us out together and had been with us all during the journey, would have become really present to those who had gathered in the Clarendon Hotel in Crystal City.

As we landed, I said to Bill, "Bill, thanks so much for coming with me. It was a wonderful trip, and what we did, we did together in Jesus' name." And I really meant it.

valuable ideas to be announced, the body quickly takes revenge by screaming loudly for affection and intimacy. Christian leaders are called to live the Incarnation, that is, to live in the body, not only in their own bodies but also in the corporate body of the community, and to discover there the presence of the Holy Spirit.

Confession and forgiveness are precisely the disciplines by which spiritualization and carnality can be avoided and true incarnation lived. Through confession, the dark powers are taken out of their carnal isolation, brought into the light, and made visible to the community. Through forgiveness, they are disarmed and dispelled and a new integration between body and spirit is made possible.

This might all sound very unrealistic, but anyone who has had any experience with healing communities such as Alcoholics Anonymous or Adult Children of Alcoholics has seen the healing power of these disciplines. Many, many Christians, priests and ministers included, have discovered the deep meaning of the Incarnation not in their churches, but in the twelve steps of A.A. and A.C.A., and have come to the awareness of God's healing presence in the confessing community of those who dare to search for healing.

All of this does not mean that ministers or priests must, explicitly, bring their own sins or failures into the pulpit or into their daily ministries. That would be unhealthy and imprudent and not at all a form of servant leadership. What it means is that ministers and priests are also called to be full members of their communities, are accountable to them and need their affection and support, and are called to minister with their whole being, including their wounded selves.

I am convinced that priests and ministers, especially those who relate to many anguishing people, need a truly safe place for themselves. They need a place where they can share their deep pain and struggles with people who do not need them, but who can guide them ever deeper into the mystery of God's love. I, personally, have been fortunate in having found such a place in L'Arche, with a group of friends who pay attention to my own often-hidden pains and keep me faithful to my vocation by their gentle criticisms and loving support. Would that all priests and ministers could have such a safe place for themselves.

III

From Leading to Being Led

*"Worship the Lord Your God,
and serve only him."*

The Temptation: To Be Powerful

Let me tell you now about a third experience connected with my move from Harvard to L'Arche. It was clearly a move from leading to being led. Somehow I had come to believe that growing older and more mature meant that I would be increasingly able to offer leadership. In fact, I had grown more self-confident over the years. I felt I knew something and had the ability to express it and be heard. In that sense I felt more and more in control.

But when I entered my community with mentally handicapped people and their assistants, all controls fell apart, and I came to realize that every hour, day, and month was full of surprises — often surprises I was least prepared for. When Bill agreed or disagreed with my sermon, he did not wait until after Mass to tell me so! Logical ideas did not receive logical responses. Often people responded from deep places in themselves, showing me that what I was saying or doing had little if anything to do with what they were living. Present feelings and emotions could no longer be held in check by beautiful words and convincing arguments. When people have little intellectual capacity, they let their hearts — their loving hearts, their angry hearts, their longing hearts — speak directly and often unadorned. Without realizing it, the people I came to live with made me aware of the extent to which my leadership was still a desire to control complex situations, confused emotions, and anxious minds.

It took me a long time to feel safe in this unpredictable climate, and I still have moments in which I clamp down and tell everyone to shut up, get in line, listen to me, and believe in what I say. But I am also getting in touch with the mystery that leadership, for a large part, means to be led. I discover that I am learning many new things, not just about the pains and struggles of wounded people, but also about their unique gifts and graces. They teach me about joy and peace, love and care and prayer — what I could never have learned in any academy. They also teach me what nobody else could have taught me, about grief and violence, fear and indifference. Most of all, they give me a glimpse of God's first love, often at moments when I start feeling depressed and discouraged.

You all know what the third temptation of Jesus was. It was the temptation of power. "I will give you all the kingdoms of this world in their splendor," the demon said to Jesus (Matthew 4:9). When I ask myself the main reason for so many people having left the church during the past decades in France, Germany, Holland, and also in Canada and America, the word "power" easily comes to mind. One of the greatest ironies of the history of Christianity is that its leaders constantly gave in to the temptation of power — political power, military power, economic power, or moral and spiritual power — even though they continued to speak in the name of Jesus, who did not cling to his divine power but emptied himself and became as we are. The temptation to consider power an apt instrument for the proclamation of the Gospel is the greatest of all. We keep hearing from others, as well as saying to ourselves, that having power — provided it is used in the service of God and your fellow human beings — is a good thing. With this rationalization, crusades took place; inquisitions were organized; Indians were enslaved; positions of great influence were desired; episcopal palaces, splendid cathedrals, and opulent seminaries were built; and much moral manipulation of conscience was engaged in. Every time we see a major crisis in the history of the church, such as the Great Schism of the eleventh century, the Reformation of the sixteenth century, or the immense secularization of the twentieth century, we always see that a major cause of rupture is the power exercised by those who claim to be followers of the poor and powerless Jesus.

What makes the temptation of power so seemingly irresistible? Maybe it is that power offers an easy substitute for the hard task of love. It seems easier to be God than to love God, easier to control people than to love people, easier to own life than to love life. Jesus asks, "Do you love me?" We ask, "Can we sit at your right hand and your left hand in your Kingdom?" (Matthew 20:21). Ever since the snake said, "The day you eat of this tree your eyes will be open and you will be like gods, knowing good from evil" (Genesis 3:5), we have been tempted to replace love with power. Jesus lived that temptation in the most agonizing way from the desert to the cross. The long painful history of the church is the history of people ever and again tempted to choose power over love, control over the cross, being a leader over

It seems easier to be God than to love God,

easier to control people than to love people,

easier to own life than to love life.

being led. Those who resisted this temptation to the end and thereby give us hope are the true saints.

One thing is clear to me: The temptation of power is greatest when intimacy is a threat. Much Christian leadership is exercised by people who do not know how to develop healthy, intimate relationships and have opted for power and control instead. Many Christian empire-builders have been people unable to give and receive love.

The Challenge:
"Somebody Else Will Take You"

Now we have to turn to Jesus again because, after having asked Peter three times if he loved him more than the others and after having commissioned him three times to be a shepherd, he said in a very emphatic way:

"In all truth I tell you
When you were young
you put on your belt
and walked where you liked;
but when you grow old
you will stretch out your hands

and somebody else will put a belt around you
and take you where you would rather not go."

(John 21:18)

These words are the words that made it possible for me to move from Harvard to L'Arche. They touch the core of Christian leadership and are spoken to offer us ever and again new ways to let go of power and follow the humble way of Jesus. The world says, "When you were young you were dependent and could not go where you wanted, but when you grow old you will be able to make your own decisions, go your own way, and control your own destiny." But Jesus has a different vision of maturity: It is the ability and willingness to be led where you would rather not go. Immediately after Peter has been commissioned to be a leader of his sheep, Jesus confronts him with the hard truth that the servant-leader is the leader who is being led to unknown, undesirable, and painful places. The way of the Christian leader is not the way of upward mobility in which our world

Jesus has a different vision of maturity: It is the ability and willingness to be led where you would rather not go.

so deeply in love with Jesus that they are ready to follow him wherever he guides them, always trusting that, with him, they will find life and find it abundantly.

The Christian leader of the future needs to be radically poor, journeying with nothing except a staff — "no bread, no haversack, no money, no spare tunic" (Mark 6:8). What is good about being poor? Nothing, except that it offers us the possibility of giving leadership by allowing ourselves to be led. We will become dependent on the positive or negative responses of those to whom we go and thus be truly led where the Spirit of Jesus wants to lead us. Wealth and riches prevent us from truly discerning the way of Jesus. Paul writes to Timothy: "People who long to be rich are a prey to trial; they get trapped into all sorts of foolish and harmful ambitions which plunge people into ruin and destruction" (1 Timothy 6:9). If there is any hope for the church in the future, it will be hope for a poor church in which its leaders are willing to be led.

The Discipline: Theological Reflection

What, then, is the discipline required of a leader who can live with outstretched hands? I propose here the discipline of strenuous theological reflection. Just as prayer keeps us connected with the first love and just as confession and forgiveness keep our ministry communal and mutual, so strenuous theological reflection will allow us to discern critically where we are being led.

Few ministers and priests think theologically. Most of us have been educated in a climate in which the behavioral sciences, such as psychology and sociology, so dominated the educational milieu that little true theology was being learned. Most Christian leaders today raise psychological or sociological questions even though they frame them in scriptural terms. Real theological thinking, which is thinking with the mind of Christ, is hard to find in the practice of the ministry. Without solid theological reflection, future leaders will be little more than pseudo-psychologists, pseudo-sociologists, pseudo-social workers. They will think of themselves as enablers, facilitators, role models, father or mother figures, big brothers or big sisters, and so on, and thus join the countless men and women who make a living by trying to help their fellow human beings cope with the stresses and strains of everyday living.

But that has little to do with Christian leadership because the Christian leader thinks, speaks, and acts in the name of Jesus, who came to free humanity from the power of death and open the way to eternal life. To be such a leader, it is essential to be able to discern from moment to moment how God acts in human history and how the personal, communal, national, and international events that occur during our lives can make us more and more sensitive to the ways in which we are led to the cross and through the cross to the resurrection.

The task of future Christian leaders is not to make a little contribution to the solution of the pains and tribulations of their time, but to identify and announce the ways in which Jesus is leading God's people out of slavery, through the desert to a new land of freedom. Christian leaders have the arduous task of responding to personal struggles, family conflicts, national calamities, and international tensions with an articulate faith in God's real presence. They have to say no to every form of fatalism, defeatism, accidentalism, or incidentalism that makes people believe that statistics are telling us the truth. They have to say no to every form of despair in which human life is seen as a pure matter of good or bad luck. They have to say no to sentimental attempts to make people develop a

[handwritten margin note:] transformative influence + Faithful presence —or— radical difference.

spirit of resignation or stoic indifference in the face of the unavoidability of pain, suffering, and death. In short, they have to say no to the secular world and proclaim in unambiguous terms that the incarnation of God's Word, through whom all things came into being, has made even the smallest event of human history into *kairos*, that is, an opportunity to be led deeper into the heart of Christ. The Christian leaders of the future have to be theologians, persons who know the heart of God and are trained — through prayer, study, and careful analysis — to manifest the divine event of God's saving work in the midst of the many seemingly random events of their time.

Theological reflection is reflecting on the painful and joyful realities of every day with the mind of Jesus and thereby raising human consciousness to the knowledge of God's gentle guidance. This is a hard discipline, since God's presence is often a hidden presence, a presence that needs to be discovered. The loud, boisterous noises of the world make us deaf to the soft, gentle, and loving

*Strenuous theological reflection will allow us
to discern critically where we are being led.*

voice of God. A Christian leader is called to help people to hear that voice and so be comforted and consoled.

Thinking about the future of Christian leadership, I am convinced that it needs to be a theological leadership. For this to come about, much — very much — has to happen in seminaries and divinity schools. They have to become centers where people are trained in true discernment of the signs of the time. This cannot be just an intellectual training. It requires a deep spiritual formation involving the whole person — body, mind, and heart. I think we are only half aware of how secular even theological schools have become. Formation in the mind of Christ, who did not cling to power but emptied himself, taking the form of a slave, is not what most seminaries are about. Everything in our competitive and ambitious world militates against it. But to the degree that such formation is being sought for and realized, there is hope for the church of the twenty-first century.

Conclusion

Let me summarize. My movement from Harvard to L'Arche made me aware in a new way how much my own thinking about Christian leadership had been affected by the desire to be relevant, the desire for popularity, and the desire for power. Too often I looked at being relevant, popular, and powerful as ingredients of an effective ministry.

The truth, however, is that these are not vocations but temptations. Jesus asks, "Do you love me?" Jesus sends us out to be shepherds, and Jesus promises a life in which we increasingly have to stretch out our hands and be led to places where we would rather not go. He asks us to move from a concern for relevance to a life of prayer, from worries about popularity to communal and mutual ministry, and from a leadership leader, the vulnerable leader, and the trusting leader. May that image fill your hearts with hope, courage, and confidence as you anticipate the new century.

Epilogue

Writing these reflections was one thing, presenting them in Washington, D.C., quite another. When Bill and I arrived at the Washington airport we were taken to the Clarendon Hotel in Crystal City, a collection of modern, seemingly all-glass high-rise buildings on the same side of the Potomac River as the airport. Both Bill and I were quite impressed by the glittering atmosphere of the hotel. We were both given spacious rooms with double beds, bathrooms with many towels, and cable TV. On the table in Bill's room there was a basket with fruit and a bottle of wine. Bill loved it. Being a veteran TV-watcher, he settled comfortably on his queen-size bed and checked out all the channels with his remote-control box.

But the time for us to bring our good news together came quickly. After a delicious buffet dinner in one of the ballrooms decorated with golden statues and little fountains, Vincent Dwyer introduced me to the audience. At that moment I still did not know what "doing it together" with Bill would mean. I opened by saying that I had not come alone, but was very happy that Bill had come with me. Then I took my handwritten text and began my address. At that moment, I saw that Bill had left his seat, walked up to the podium, and planted himself right behind me. It was clear that he had a much more concrete idea about the meaning of "doing it together" than I. Each time I finished reading a page, he took it away and put it upside down on a small table close by. I felt very much at ease with this and started to feel Bill's presence as a support.

But Bill had more in mind. When I began to speak about the temptation to turn stones into bread as a temptation to be relevant, he interrupted me and said loudly for everyone to hear, "I have heard that before!" He had indeed, and he

"And we did it together,

didn't we?"

just wanted the priests and ministers who were listening to know that he knew me quite well and was familiar with my ideas. For me, however, it felt like a gentle loving reminder that my thoughts were not as new as I wanted my audience to believe. Bill's intervention created a new atmosphere in the ballroom: lighter, easier, and more playful. Somehow Bill had taken away the seriousness of the occasion and had brought to it some homespun normality. As I continued my presentation, I felt more and more that we were indeed doing it together. And it felt good.

When I came to the second part and was reading the words, "The question most asked by the handicapped people with whom I live was, 'Are you home tonight?'" Bill interrupted me again and said, "That's right, that is what John Smeltzer always asks." Again there was something disarming about his remark. Bill knew John Smeltzer very well after living with him in the same house for quite some years. He simply wanted people to know about his friend. It was as if he drew the audience toward us, inviting them into the intimacy of our common life.

After I had finished reading my text and people had shown their appreciation, Bill said to me, "Henri, can I say something now?" My first reaction was, "Oh, how am I going to handle this? He might start rambling and create an embarrassing situation," but then I caught myself in my presumption that he had nothing of importance to say and said to the audience, "Will you please sit down? Bill would like to say a few words to you."

Bill took the microphone and said, with all the difficulties he has in speaking, "Last time, when Henri went to Boston, he took John Smeltzer with him. This time he wanted me to come with him to Washington, and I am very glad to be here with you. Thank you very much." That was it, and everyone stood up and gave him warm applause.

As we walked away from the podium, Bill said to me, "Henri, how did you like my speech?"

"Very much," I answered. "Everyone was really happy with what you said." Bill was delighted. As people gathered for drinks, he felt freer than ever. He went from person to person, introduced himself, asked how they liked the evening, and told them all sorts of stories about his life in Daybreak. I did not see him for more than an hour. He was too busy getting to know everybody.

The next morning at breakfast before we left, Bill walked from table to table with his cup of coffee in his hands and said goodbye to all those he knew from the evening before. It was clear to me that he had made many friends and felt very much at home in these, for him, so unusual surroundings.

As we flew back together to Toronto, Bill looked up from the word-puzzle book that he takes with him wherever he goes and said, "Henri, did you like our trip?"

"Oh, yes," I answered, "it was a wonderful trip, and I am so glad you came with me."

Study Guide

Introduction

Nouwen asks himself "Did becoming older bring me closer to Jesus?" Reflect on this question for your own life.

1. From Relevance to Prayer

a. *The Temptation: To Be Relevant*

"Jesus' first temptation was to be relevant." Have you ever experienced this temptation in your own ministry?

b. *The Question: "Do You Love Me?"*

"Are you in love with Jesus"? Answer Nouwen's question for your own life.

"You are loved without any conditions or limits." Have you ever found it hard to accept that God loved you in this way?

Take a moment to imagine and feel the immensity of God's unconditional love.

c. *The Discipline: Contemplative Prayer*

"Christian leadership must be rooted in the permanent, intimate relationship with the incarnate Word, Jesus, and they need to find there the source for their words, advice, and guidance." Imagine a conversation taking place about some of the political and moral "burning issues" Nouwen refers to on page 44. How do these conversations usually take place? Now imagine how they could be different if based on "the experience of God's first love" and rooted in the experience of contemplative prayer.

2. From Popularity to Ministry

a. *The Temptation: To Be Spectacular*

Have people ever expected you to be a superman or superwoman, solving every problem on your own? How did you respond to these expectations?

b. *The Task: "Feed My Sheep"*

"It is Jesus who heals, not I; Jesus who speaks words of truth, not I; Jesus who is Lord, not I." According to Nouwen, how is a Jesus-centered view of leadership different from the leadership exercised by a psychologist or doctor?

c. *The Discipline: Confession and Forgiveness*

"Ministers and priests ... are called to minister with their whole being, including their wounded selves." Reflect on appropriate ways you can more fully open yourself to your community.

3. *From Leading to Being Led*

    a. *The Temptation: To Be Powerful*

"It seems easier to be God than to love God." Describe in your own words what this means. Why do you think it is sometimes hard for us to love God?

    b. *The Challenge:*
    "Someone Else Will Take You"

"Jesus has a different vision of maturity: It is the ability and willingness to be led where you would rather not go." Think of the last time God was calling you to make a change in your life. Was it difficult to let go of your own wishes and follow God's direction?

    c. *The Discipline: Theological Reflection*

On page 44, Nouwen describes theology as "union with God in prayer." How is theological reflection different from psychological or scientific investigation?

"The Christian leader thinks, speaks, and acts in the name of Jesus." Can you think of three specific ways your own vocation can be enriched by teaching "in the name of Jesus"? How can you integrate prayer as part of this direction?